MOON EXPLORATION
FACT AND FANTASY

Bruce LaFontaine

Dover Publications, Inc.
Mineola, New York

Planet Friendly Publishing
✔ Made in the United States
✔ Printed on Recycled Paper
Text: 30%   Cover: 10%
Learn more: www.greenedition.org

At Dover Publications we're committed to producing books in an earth-friendly manner and to helping our customers make greener choices.

Manufacturing books in the United States ensures compliance with strict environmental laws and eliminates the need for international freight shipping, a major contributor to global air pollution.

And printing on recycled paper helps minimize our consumption of trees, water and fossil fuels. The text of *Moon Exploration Fact and Fantasy* was printed on paper made with 30% post-consumer waste, and the cover was printed on paper made with 10% post-consumer waste. According to Environmental Defense's Paper Calculator, by using this innovative paper instead of conventional papers, we achieved the following environmental benefits:

Trees Saved: 5 • Air Emissions Eliminated: 389 pounds
Water Saved: 1,731 gallons • Solid Waste Eliminated: 205 pounds

For more information on our environmental practices, please visit us online at www.doverpublications.com/green

ABOUT THE AUTHOR

Bruce LaFontaine is the writer and illustrator of thirty-five non-fiction children's books. He specializes in the subject areas of history, science, transportation, and architecture for middle readers, ages eight through twelve. Mr. LaFontaine's published works include *Modern Experimental Aircraft, Famous Buildings of Frank Lloyd Wright, Great Inventors and Inventions*, and many others. His book, *Exploring the Solar System*, published in 1999, was selected by *Astronomy* magazine as one of the twenty-one best astronomy books for children. In the same year, Mr. LaFontaine was profiled in *Something About the Author*, a hardcover publication featuring prominent authors and illustrators in the field of children's literature. He has worked in the Rochester, New York area as a writer, illustrator, and art director for twenty-five years.

Bibliographical Note

Moon Exploration Fact and Fantasy is a new work, first published by Dover Publications, Inc., in 2001.

DOVER *Pictorial Archive* SERIES

This book belongs to the Dover Pictorial Archive Series. You may use the designs and illustrations for graphics and crafts applications, free and without special permission, provided that you include no more than four in the same publication or project. (For permission for additional use, please write to Permissions Department, Dover Publications, Inc., 31 East 2nd Street, Mineola, N.Y. 11501.)

However, republication or reproduction of any illustration by any other graphic service, whether it be in a book or in any other design resource, is strictly prohibited.

International Standard Book Number
ISBN-13: 978-0-486-41549-9
ISBN-10: 0-486-41549-X

Manufactured in the United States by Courier Corporation
41549X02
www.doverpublications.com

INTRODUCTION

In its nightly procession across the evening skies, the moon exerts an influence both real and imagined on our planet earth and its inhabitants. Its size, brightness, and proximity has fascinated human beings since the dawn of time. The moon has been observed, studied, written about, and even visited by our curious species, yet remains to us an imposing and mysterious celestial body.

Early civilizations considered the moon to be an embodiment of one of their many mythical gods, endowed with strange and magical properties. Moon symbols have been discovered in carved stone tablets dating back to the ancient empire of Babylon, around 1700 B.C. Stories about the moon have become part of our history, beginning with Greek writings from its classical period (around 300 B.C.). In Greek myths, the moon goddess and sister of the sun god Helios is named "Selene," a word that became the basis of the prefix for terms that apply to the study of the physical moon, like selenography and selenophysics, as well as to selenology, the branch of astronomy that deals specifically with the moon. The Romans worshipped the moon goddess "Luna," the origin of the word "lunar." The literature of the medieval period also abounds with tales about the moon.

The scientific study of the moon began in the late Renaissance period with the great astronomer Galileo Galilei. In 1610, Galileo made the first—and surprisingly accurate—drawings of the lunar surface by observing it through a telescope of his own construction. He described mountains, craters, and large dark areas that looked like seas. We now know that these dark prominent markings, which give rise to its "man in the moon" appearance, are actually huge basins filled in by a smooth layer of lava from the moon's interior.

During the nineteenth century, the moon became the object of fantasy and romance literature. The two great pioneers of modern science fiction, Jules Verne (1828–1905) and H. G. Wells (1866–1946), both wrote novels about moon travel that have become classics—Verne with *From the Earth to the Moon* (1865) and Wells with *The First Men in the Moon* (1901). In turn, this new literary genre became the inspiration for generations of astronomers who applied the methods of science and the tools of technology to the study of the moon. Finally, with the invention of motion pictures in the early part of the twentieth century, the moon became a popular subject in science fiction films. From 1902 until the present day, sci-fi movies have run the gamut in their depiction of the moon—ranging from vivid documentary-style realism to the realm of pure fantasy.

(continued)

Beginning in the late 1950s, the moon came under much more intense scientific scrutiny as we entered the era of the "space age." Unmanned robotic probes reached the moon, photographed its formerly unseen dark side, and even landed on the lunar surface. This exploration culminated in July, 1969 with the historic landing of two American astronauts on the moon from the lunar module of *Apollo 11*. During the next four years, five more *Apollo* moon missions would be launched by the United States. *Apollo* explorers set up instruments on the lunar surface, collected samples that were brought back to earth, and even drove a "moon-mobile" across its dusty plains.

In recent years, two unmanned American lunar spacecraft have collected tantalizing new data suggesting the presence of frozen water on the moon, a discovery that—if confirmed—has important implications for colonizing the moon. For one thing, it would mean that future explorers and settlers there would have a supply of breathable oxygen and drinking water processed from "moon ice," greatly facilitating the establishment of permanent lunar bases. For another, lunar explorers could manufacture rocket fuel by chemically separating water into its two constituent elements, hydrogen and oxygen—the principal ingredients of rocket fuel.

In the near future, there will undoubtedly be manned missions to the moon. By mid-century, permanent bases for scientific study, mining, and colonization may dot the face of the lunar surface. Our nearest neighbor in space may also serve as the springboard for further planetary exploration, especially of Mars, the red planet. As we obtain more and more scientific data about the moon, we learn more about how our own planet was formed. But regardless of the depth and extent of our factual knowledge, the moon will always be a source of beauty and awe, as we continue to gaze upward and contemplate the brilliant glow of the earth's inscrutable companion.

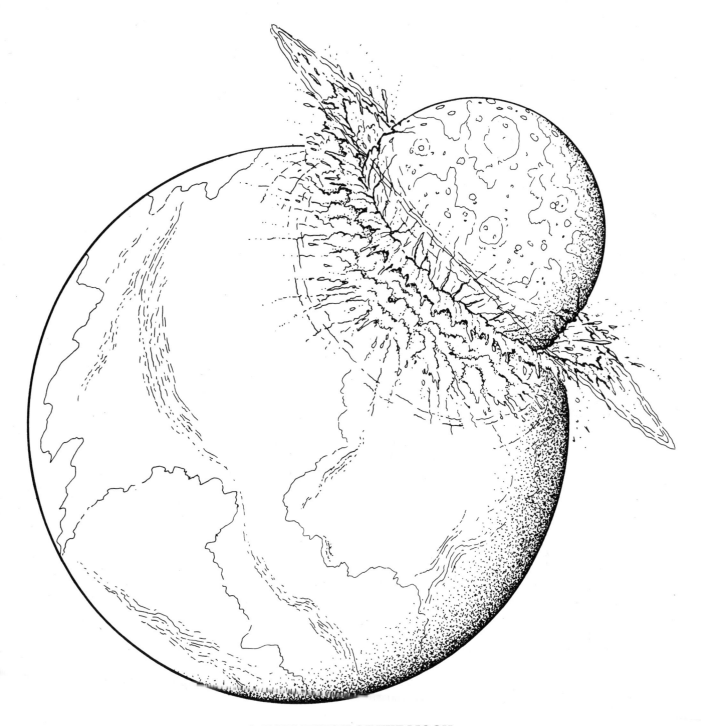

1. FORMATION OF THE MOON

The question of how the moon became our closest neighbor in space has been the subject of scientific inquiry for generations of astronomers. Although the age of the earth has been generally established at around 4.5 billion years, details about the moon's formation and age are less clear. In the twentieth century, three theories about the birth of the moon have been discussed and debated.

One theory postulates that in the very early stages of our solar system, gases composed of the basic elements whirled around our parent star, the sun. Over billions of years, individual swirls of these gases condensed into the planets we know today. Around each planet, additional gas swirls eventually coalesced into their moons. This is known as the "nebula theory." Another closely related idea, the "daughter theory," suggests that the moon was once a part of the ancient earth. Because the newly formed earth was still spinning very rapidly, a portion of the planet was spun off into orbit to become the moon.

A rather different explanation for the moon's formation is

the "capture theory." This supposes that the moon was formed as a separate planet orbiting the sun. Due to an eccentric orbit, the moon came too close to the powerful gravity of earth and was captured, becoming an orbiting satellite of our planet.

Currently, the most widely accepted idea explaining the birth of the moon is the "impact theory." As shown in the above illustration, scientists now believe that the earth was struck by a large "planetesimal," a celestial body perhaps as large as the planet Mars. This occurred between 4.2 and 3.9 billion years ago. The force of this massive impact blew billions of tons of the primitive earth into space. Over millions of years, this debris formed into a ring orbiting the earth, much like the visible ring system of the planet Saturn. As more millennia of time passed, the rings clumped into small "moonlets" from gravitational attraction. Eventually, after the passage of many more millions of years, these moonlets were drawn together by gravity into a single sphere—the moon we see today.

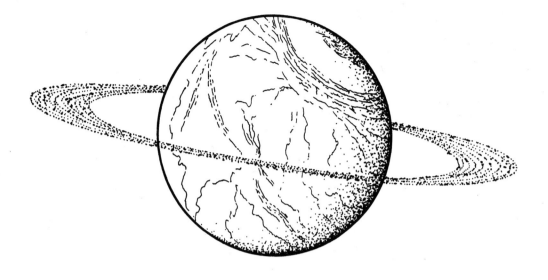

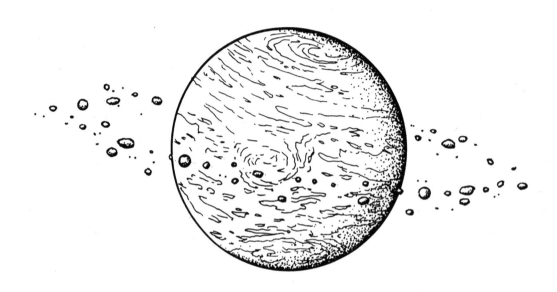

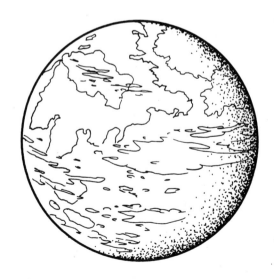

2. THE IMPACT THEORY OF LUNAR FORMATION

The above illustration depicts the ring system formed from the debris of the original collision of the earth with another large planetary body. Over millions of years, the ring material clumped together into small individual moonlets orbiting the earth. These moonlets were eventually drawn into a single orbiting sphere by gravity, thus taking the form of our familiar moon.

3. SIZE COMPARISON OF THE EARTH AND MOON, AND THE MOON AND THE UNITED STATES

Our moon circles the earth in an elliptical orbit at 2,300 miles per hour, at a distance of 252,698 miles away. The fifth largest planetary satellite in the solar system, it is exceeded only by the planet-sized moons of giant Jupiter and Saturn. It is in fact the largest moon in our solar system in relation to the size of its planet. With a diameter of 2,159 miles, the moon is slightly over one-quarter the size of the earth, whose diameter is 7,927 miles. The moon is almost as large as the width of the continental United States, a distance of 2,400 miles as measured from New York City to San Francisco.

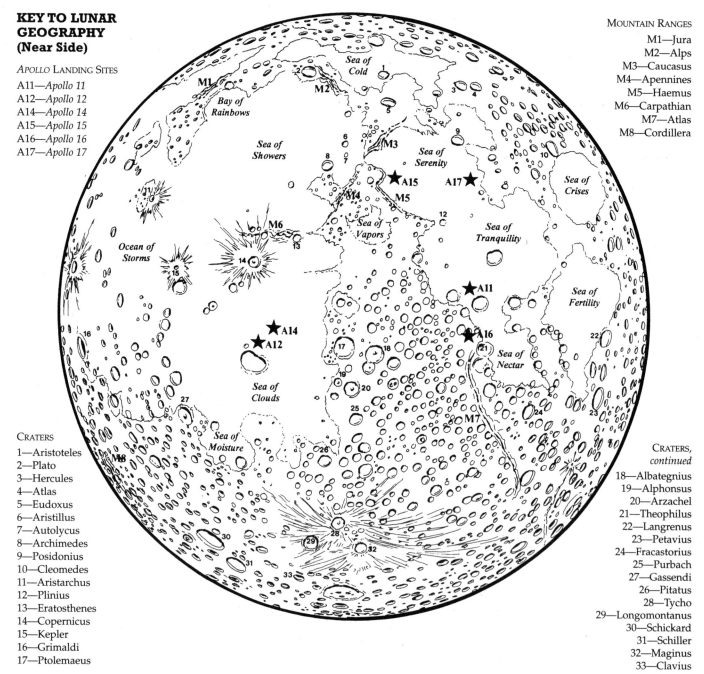

4. GEOGRAPHY OF THE NEAR (EARTH-FACING) SIDE OF THE MOON

Although the earth's human inhabitants have been gazing at the moon for thousands of years, we have only ever been able to see one side, or hemisphere, of the lunar world. This is due to an odd coincidence. The time that it takes for the moon to complete one full rotation on its axis is exactly equal to the time needed for the moon to accomplish one full orbit around the earth, a period of twenty-seven days, seven hours, and forty-three minutes, or roughly one month. That is why only one side of the moon is visible from earth. It was not until October 1959, when the Soviet spacecraft *Luna 3* circled and photographed the moon, that we were first able to glimpse its far side.

The near side as shown above is distinguished by several prominent surface features. Most apparent are the large irregularly shaped dark areas called "maria," which is Latin for seas ("mare" for sea). These are huge basins on the lunar surface which have been filled with a smooth coating of dark basalt rock, now solidified. This material flowed up as lava from the molten interior of the moon through cracks and fissures in the early lunar crust between 3.8 and 3.2 billion years ago. The largest of the lunar seas, the Sea of Showers (or Mare Imbrium) spans 750 miles—about the size

of the state of Texas—and covers an area of 340,000 square miles. Other large seas are the Sea of Tranquility at 600 miles, and the Sea of Fertility at 430 miles in diameter. The moon also has a number of high mountain ranges, with some peaks as high or higher than those on the earth. Mountains on the near side include the Apennines, the Alps, the Caucasus, the Atlas, the Carpathians, as well as several others.

The other significant feature of lunar geology is the thousands of impact craters that pockmark its surface. There are more than 30,000 craters on the moon's near side that have been mapped and identified. The largest craters are named after famous scientists and philosophers. The crater Clavius has a diameter of 140 miles. Other large craters are Plato at 63 miles and Atlas at 55 miles. Several large craters have prominent white streaks emanating from them, and are known as "ray craters." Tycho—55 miles wide—has rays that range over 1,000 miles. Copernicus, 57 miles wide, lies at the hub of one of the most extensive ray systems on the moon. These bright rays are composed of lighter colored material ejected from the crater when they were formed by meteoric impact.

MOUNTAIN RANGES
M1—Cordillera
M2—Rook

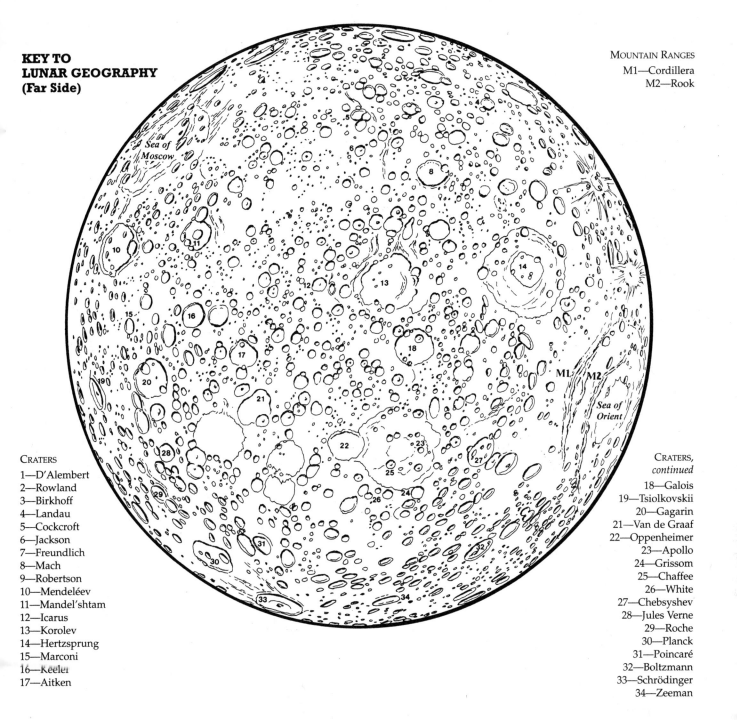

CRATERS
1—D'Alembert
2—Rowland
3—Birkhoff
4—Landau
5—Cockcroft
6—Jackson
7—Freundlich
8—Mach
9—Robertson
10—Mendeléev
11—Mandel'shtam
12—Icarus
13—Korolev
14—Hertzsprung
15—Marconi
16—Keeler
17—Aitken

CRATERS,
continued
18—Galois
19—Tsiolkovskii
20—Gagarin
21—Van de Graaf
22—Oppenheimer
23—Apollo
24—Grissom
25—Chaffee
26—White
27—Chebsyshev
28—Jules Verne
29—Roche
30—Planck
31—Poincaré
32—Boltzmann
33—Schrödinger
34—Zeeman

5. GEOGRAPHY OF THE FAR SIDE OF THE MOON

The side of the moon hidden from view is markedly different from the visible one. It has fewer and smaller maria (or seas), but is riddled with many more craters. In its early history, the amount of cratering on the moon was greater than at the present time, because billions of years ago both the earth and moon experienced a much higher level of bombardment by meteors and other space debris remaining from the formation of the solar system. One of the large dark sea areas is Mare Orientale (Sea of Orient) shown on the lower right edge of the moon in the above illustration. An impact crater rather than a flat lava plain, it is different from the maria on the near side. Formed over 3 billion years ago, it has a bull's-eye appearance caused by rings of mountains around its edges that were created from the initial impact and ejected material. Mare Orientale has a diameter of 600 miles to its outermost mountain range. The Cordillera and Rook mountains form part of the ring around Mare Orientale. A large crater in the center of the illustration, Korolev, has a diameter of 52 miles, and was named for the famous Russian rocket scientist Sergei Korolev.

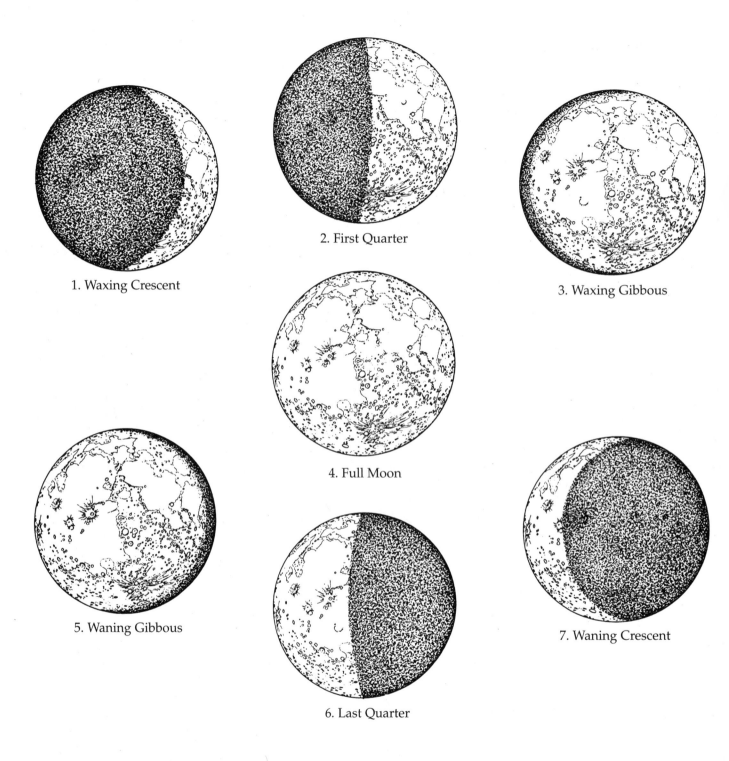

1. Waxing Crescent

2. First Quarter

3. Waxing Gibbous

4. Full Moon

5. Waning Gibbous

6. Last Quarter

7. Waning Crescent

6. PHASES OF THE MOON

As we view the moon in the night sky, its appearance alters from week to week. These changes are called phases. A complete cycle of these changes occurs every month. This regular lunar sequence is caused by the way in which our view of the sunlit portion of the moon alters as the moon circles around the earth in its month-long orbit. The moon's phases begin with the "new moon," which is in complete darkness and not visible from earth, followed by a sliver of illuminated lunar surface called a "waxing crescent." The next phase is the "first quarter," followed by a "waxing gibbous" phase (the word "gibbous" comes from the Latin word meaning "a hump" or "bulging")—wherein most of the moon is illuminated. This is followed by the familiar "full moon" phase. As it progresses in its monthly cycle, the moon enters a "waning gibbous" phase, a "last quarter" phase followed by the "waning crescent" moon, and returning finally to a no longer visible "new moon."

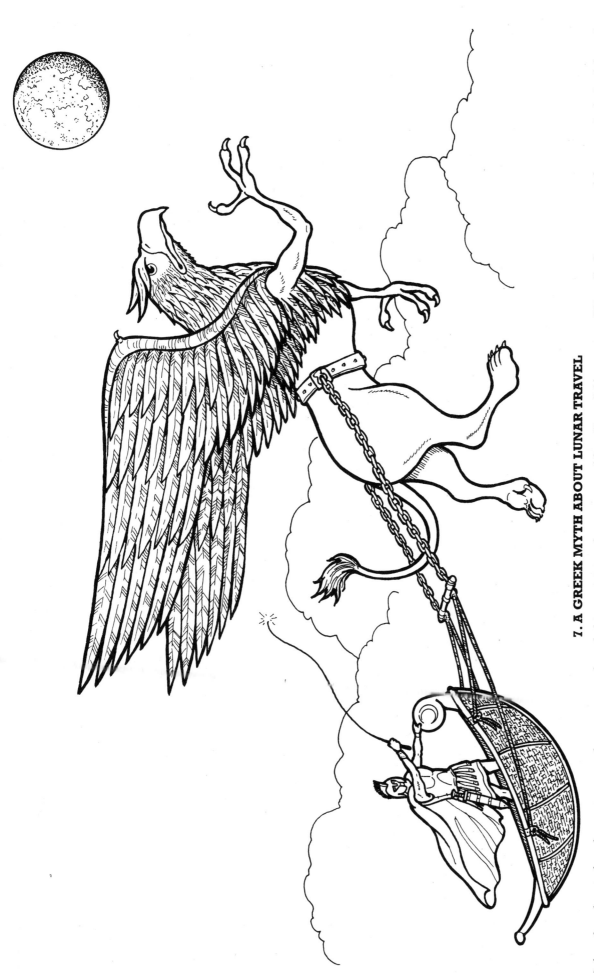

7. A GREEK MYTH ABOUT LUNAR TRAVEL

Before the advent of modern astronomy, the moon was shrouded in mystery and was regarded with awe by our ancient ancestors. Many myths, legends, and folk tales have been recorded during the 5,000 years of our civilization's history. Stone tablets from the Babylonian city of Uruk have been discovered with clear images of the moon carved into them. Scientists and philosophers from ancient Egypt, Greece, Persia, and Rome all wrote about the mysterious world that they observed in the night sky. The moon goddess of the Greeks was known as "Selene," while the Romans called the moon after their goddess "Luna" (the same as "Diana"). Our own word for moon is derived from the Anglo-Saxon "mona," a cousin of the German "mond." The picture above is based on a legend from ancient Greece, and shows Alexander the Great traveling to the moon in a boat-shaped chariot pulled by a griffin, a mythical beast. This legendary animal had the body and hindquarters of a lion, and the wings and head of an eagle, and recurred throughout Western mythology from the time of the ancients to the Middle Ages.

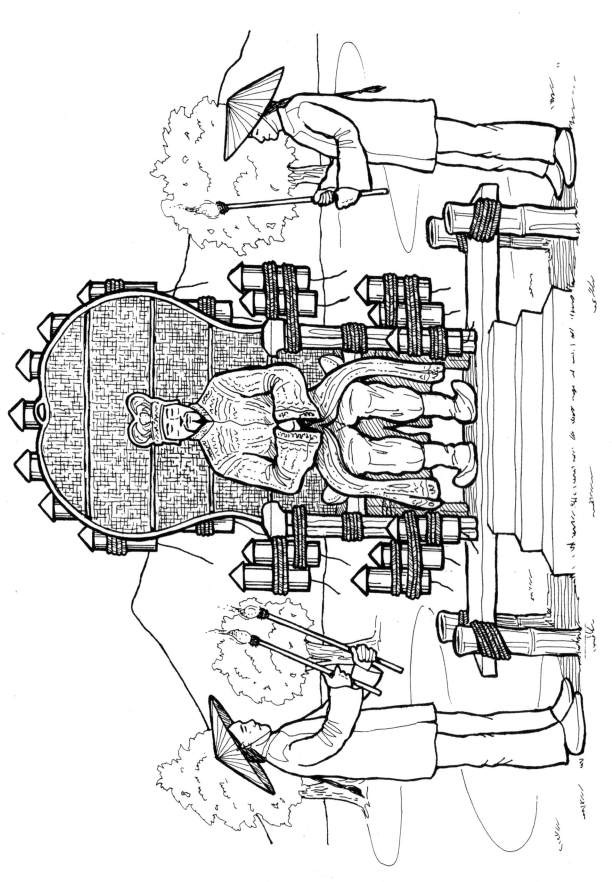

8. CHINESE LEGEND OF WAN HU

While many myths and fanciful stories about the moon come from Western literature, the great civilization of ancient China also had its share. One story dating from around 3000 B.C. concerns a venerable Chinese inventor, Wan Hu. According to the legend, Wan Hu attached forty-seven firecrackers to a chair in an attempt to blast himself to the moon. Perhaps the tale of the rocket chair was somehow related to the fact that the Chinese invented gunpowder. In any event, when all the firecrackers were ignited by Wan Hu's assistants, the adventurous mandarin disappeared in a ball of fire and was never heard from again.

9. CYRANO DE BERGERAC'S DEW CUPS

Cyrano de Bergerac (1619–1655) was a well-known French playwright and satirist who wrote several stories concerning methods of traveling from the earth to the moon. Pictured above is his idea for rising from the surface of the earth toward the moon using cups of morning dew attached to his waist. Cyrano reasoned that since the early morning dew rises (evaporates) into the air, why shouldn't a person be lifted upwards by the rising dew? A very long stretch of logic, but a charming one nonetheless.

10. CYRANO DE BERGERAC'S CONVECTION BOX

Cyrano also wrote about a traveling conveyance that was based more on scientific principles than were his dew cups. The illustration above shows a possible design for a "convection box" lifting device. It is based on the principle that air warmed by the sun rises. His box had openings on the bottom and top for air to enter and exit. As cool air entered the bottom and passed through the box, it would be warmed by the sun's rays coming into an opening on the side of the box. This method of heating is called "convection." The warmed air would exit through the top openings where it would be captured by a large sail, causing the box to be propelled upward. Although this basic principle was correct, the technology of Cyrano's day was far too primitive to transform his idea into reality.

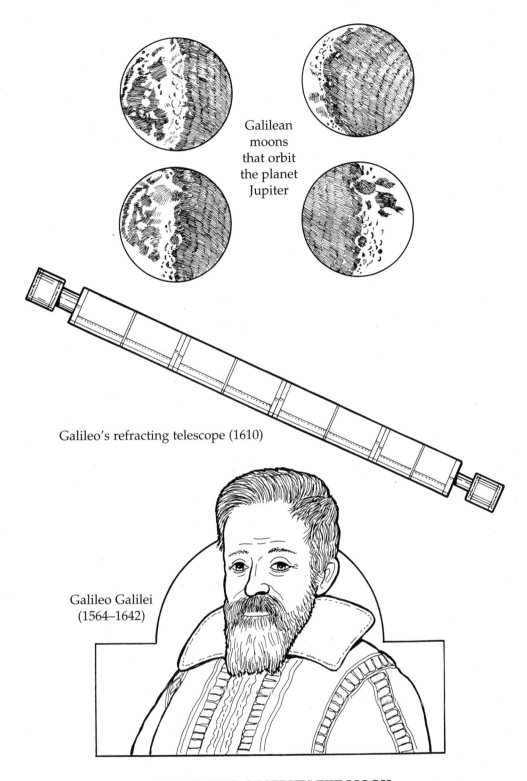

Galilean moons that orbit the planet Jupiter

Galileo's refracting telescope (1610)

Galileo Galilei
(1564–1642)

11. GALILEO OBSERVES THE MOON

The great Italian mathematical physicist Galileo Galilei was the first astronomer to observe and study the moon using a telescope. Although this instrument had been invented in 1608 by Dutch optician Hans Lippershey (c. 1570–1619), Galileo constructed his own telescope in 1609. Using this device, he viewed the moon and made accurate drawings of its surface features, correctly reporting the existence of mountains and craters on the lunar landscape. Galileo is also credited with discovering four large moons orbiting the giant planet Jupiter. These planet-sized celestial bodies are now known as the "Galilean moons" (shown on page 44 of this book in a size comparison with our own moon).

During Galileo's time it was a widely held belief that the earth was the center of the universe, around which the sun and all other stars and planets orbited—a notion based on the writings of the ancient Greek astronomer Ptolemy. This belief was strongly embraced by the Catholic Church, a powerful religious and political institution of the period. In 1543, the brilliant Polish astronomer Nicolas Copernicus (1473–1543) correctly deduced—without the aid of a telescope—that our earth revolved around the sun, thereby directly contradicting the Church's teachings. As an outspoken champion of the Copernican heliocentric theory, Galileo was put on trial for heresy—i.e., religious treason. He was threatened with execution unless he publicly recanted his beliefs, which he wisely chose to do. But his trial had set the stage for other astronomers to examine the work of Copernicus, and within a few short years, the scientific community widely supported the idea of a sun-centered solar system.

12. LUNAR CRATERS

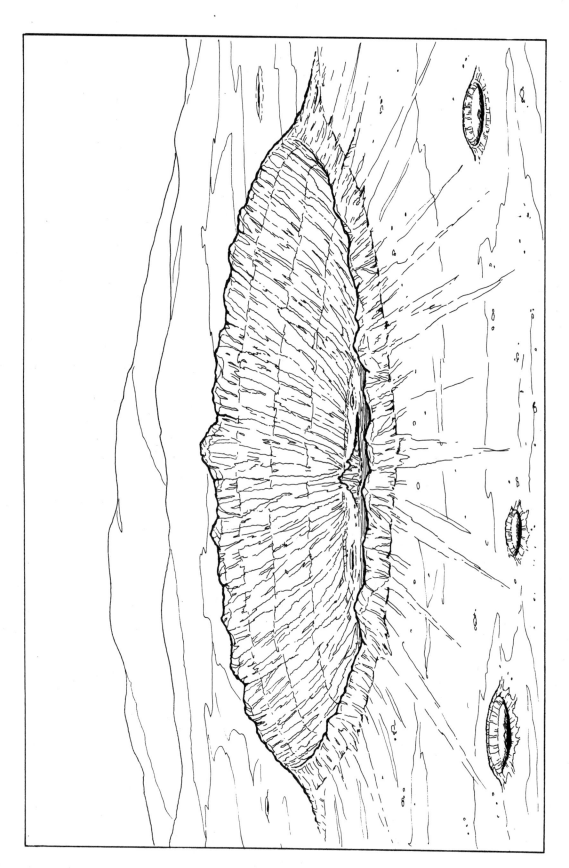

There are more than 30,000 craters on the near side of the moon. They are the by-product of billions of years of impacts on the lunar surface by meteors, asteroids, comets, and other space debris. The earth has also been bombarded with thousands of impacts during that period, but weathering by wind, rain, and other geological activity has largely erased signs of the earth's battering. There are very few obvious and intact meteor craters currently visible on our planet.

On the other hand, because there is no water and wind erosion on the airless moon, and because it is relatively geologically inactive, the scars of meteoric impact there have been preserved for millions of years. Many of these craters are over 100 miles in diam-

eter and thousands of feet deep. Theophilus, a crater 62 miles wide, has inside walls that rise 17,000 feet from the floor of the crater. The deepest crater, Newton, has walls that reach 29,000 feet from the bottom of the crater. However, the outside walls of these massive depressions usually rise to only 1,000 or 2,000 feet above the moon's actual outer surface. Many large craters have small mountains or hills located at their centers caused by the ejected rock material blasted out by the original impact explosion. This debris eventually falls back to the lunar surface, most of it forming the mountainous crater walls, while a portion settles at the center of the crater.

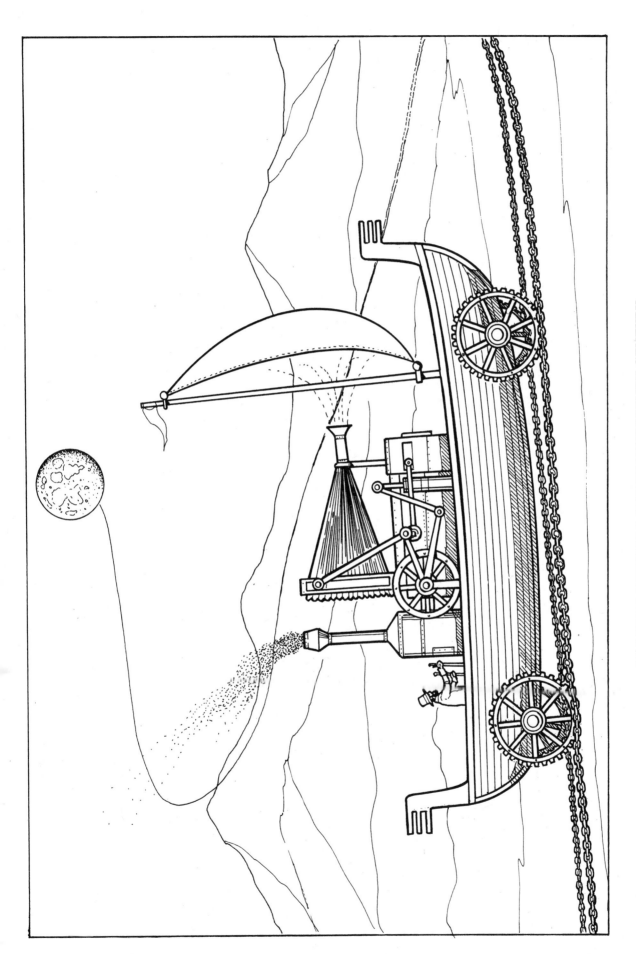

13. LUNAR GONDOLA OF THE NINETEENTH CENTURY

During the nineteenth century, the world became more and more integrated into the "machine age." Novel ideas for travel to the moon were widespread. From Italy came a suggestion to use a Venetian canal "gondola" equipped with a steam-powered bellows blowing air into a sail. The boat would be fitted with wheels resembling gears, while the teeth of the geared wheels would fit into tracks made of chain that stretched from the earth to the moon. Travelers could then ride the gondola along the metallic lunar highway. How to first construct and position the chains to the moon was not mentioned in this fanciful plan.

14.–15. GREAT LUNAR HOAX OF 1835

Tales of a fantastic lunar civilization were spread by a series of newspaper articles appearing in the *New York Sun*, beginning on August 25, 1835 when British-born essayist Richard Adams Locke (1800–1871) wrote entirely fabricated stories about the discoveries made by Sir John Herschel (1792–1871), a well-known and respected British astronomer of the day. Locke reported that Herschel had constructed an enormous telescope with a lens fully twenty-four feet in diameter—even larger than the biggest telescopes of today. From his observatory, Herschel was supposed to have seen clearly many details of life on the moon, including cities with huge obelisks and pyramids, and inhabitants resembling orange-furred orangutans who were able to fly using their bat-like wings. Locke wrote these stories with great

The
New York ☀ Sun
New York City, New York

1835

Price Five Cents

MOON CREATURES SEEN!
Famed Astronomer Discovers Lunar Civilization

Story by
Richard Adams Locke

verisimilitude, as if reporting on actual scientific discoveries; he claimed as his source an advance copy of the *Edinburgh Journal of Science* (which was in truth long defunct), where the data was allegedly first published. Almost overnight, the circulation of the *Sun* skyrocketed from 8,000 to over 19,000 readers, making it suddenly the world's largest newspaper. Sir John Herschel, who was far away in Cape Town, South Africa doing astronomical research at the time, knew noth-

ing of the deceit or his alleged connection with it until the incident was past. The installments continued until August 31, 1835, when Locke's editors at the newspaper discovered the hoax and revealed the truth about their fictional basis. Nonetheless, the idea of intelligent lunar beings was planted in the public imagination, there to be mined by fiction writers throughout the nineteenth and twentieth centuries.

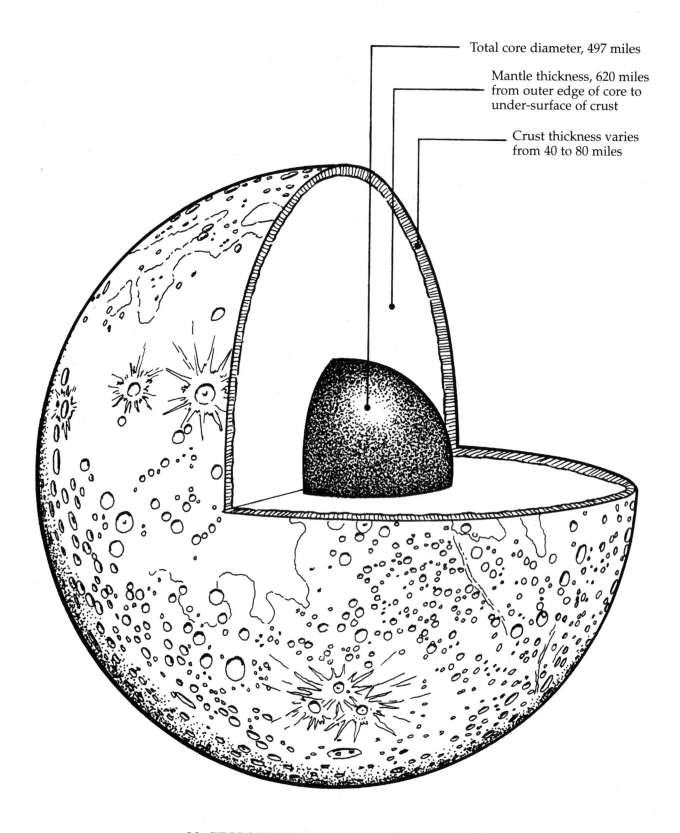

Total core diameter, 497 miles

Mantle thickness, 620 miles from outer edge of core to under-surface of crust

Crust thickness varies from 40 to 80 miles

16. GEOLOGY OF THE MOON'S INNER STRUCTURE

Much like the earth, our moon has three distinct geological layers beneath its surface—the crust, the mantle, and the core—but that is where the similarity ends. The earth is still a geologically active planet with a molten metallic core characterized by such phenomena as volcanoes, hot springs, earthquakes, and a magnetic field which surrounds it. The moon has long been a cold world, with an outer core comprised of partly molten silicates, and a tiny metallic inner core—possibly consisting of iron—in total approximately 497 miles in diameter. Surrounding the core is the thickest layer—the mantle—believed to be 620 miles thick from the core to the moon's crustal layer, composed of a dark-colored solid basalt rock material. The outer lunar surface—the crust—varies in thickness from 40 to 80 miles. It is thinner on the earth-facing side than on the far side. The crust is composed of light colored rock called anorthosites, which give the lunar highlands their bright color, and is much like granite on earth.

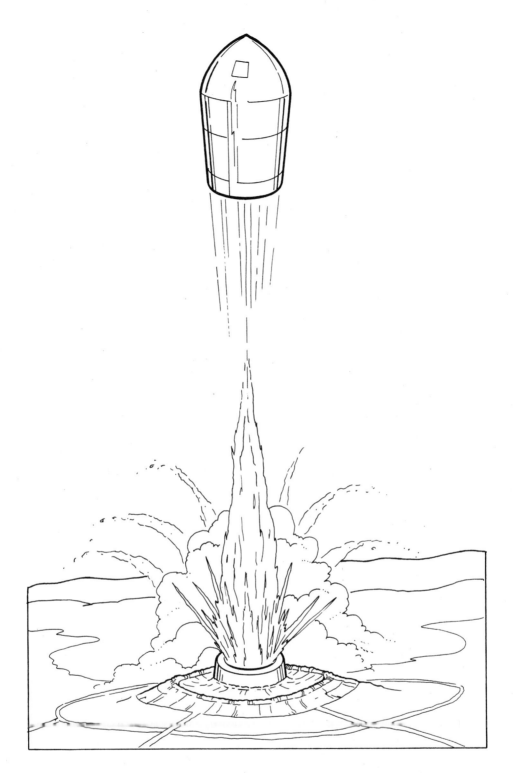

17. JULES VERNE'S *FROM THE EARTH TO THE MOON*

One of the most successful and prolific writers of the late nineteenth century was French novelist Jules Verne, whose adventure stories featured exotic locations, thrilling adventures—and especially—futuristic machines. He is widely regarded as the father of the science fiction genre of literature. Verne wrote about giant airships able to fly vast distances at great altitudes, the fabulous submarine *Nautilus* commanded by the mysterious Captain Nemo, and a daring journey to the center of the earth. Verne had the uncanny gift of being able to anticipate the future as he conceived it in his fictional tales.

One of Verne's most popular books is *From the Earth to the Moon* (1865), a novel which had a solid basis in the known scientific facts of the day. For example, he correctly deduced the speed necessary for a spacecraft to escape the earth's gravity—i.e., 12,000 yards per second—and the optimum

launching site, Tampa, Florida, only a short distance from today's Cape Canaveral. The story, set shortly after the end of the Civil War, centers around three wealthy gentlemen of the Baltimore area (in fact, the book is subtitled *The Baltimore Gun Club*) who decide to construct a gigantic cannon with the capability of sending an artillery shell all the way to the moon. After many trials and tribulations, the group finally succeeds in building a 900 foot-long cannon with walls six feet thick. To propel the artillery shell, they use a mysterious and ultra-powerful explosive of their own concoction. The group's intention shifts during the course of the novel from merely hitting the moon with a projectile, to actually traveling to the moon within a specially designed hollow shell-like ship. The novel ends at the moment of firing the great cannon. The action continues in the sequel, *Around the Moon and Back Again* (1870).

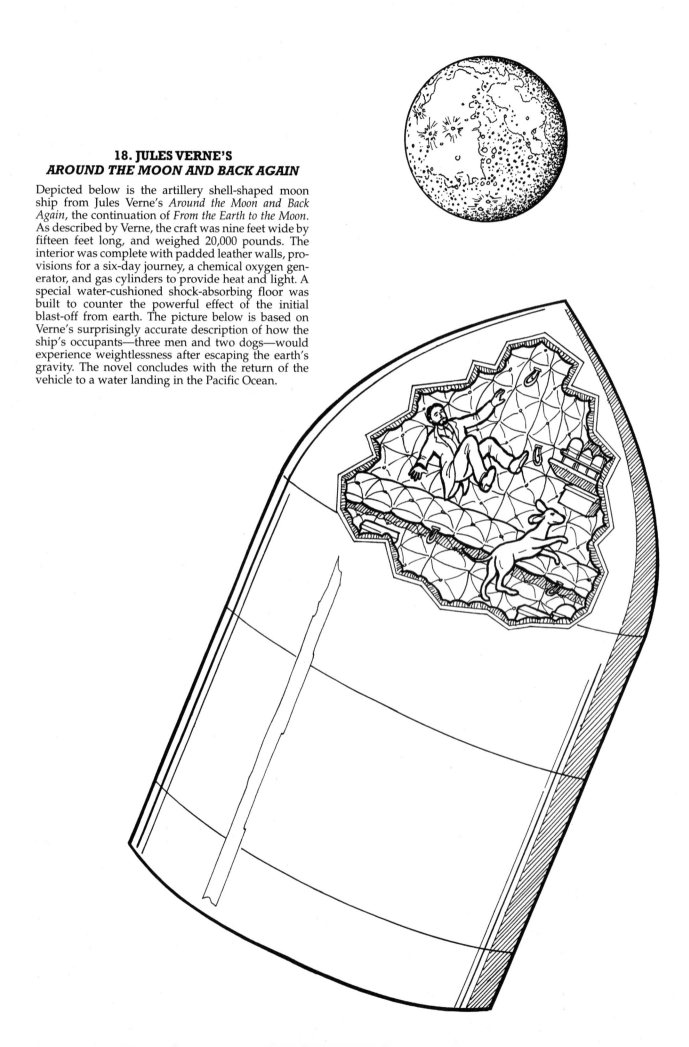

18. JULES VERNE'S
AROUND THE MOON AND BACK AGAIN

Depicted below is the artillery shell-shaped moon ship from Jules Verne's *Around the Moon and Back Again*, the continuation of *From the Earth to the Moon*. As described by Verne, the craft was nine feet wide by fifteen feet long, and weighed 20,000 pounds. The interior was complete with padded leather walls, provisions for a six-day journey, a chemical oxygen generator, and gas cylinders to provide heat and light. A special water-cushioned shock-absorbing floor was built to counter the powerful effect of the initial blast-off from earth. The picture below is based on Verne's surprisingly accurate description of how the ship's occupants—three men and two dogs—would experience weightlessness after escaping the earth's gravity. The novel concludes with the return of the vehicle to a water landing in the Pacific Ocean.

19. H. G. WELLS' *THE FIRST MEN IN THE MOON*

The other great voice in science fiction to emerge at the end of the nineteenth century was the English writer H. G. Wells. Like Jules Verne, he had an eerie ability to anticipate the future in his novels. Before their invention, Wells wrote about the powerful role that aircraft and tanks would play in wars of the future. Two of his novels, *The Time Machine* and *War of the Worlds*, have become classics of world literature.

Shown above is a scene from his 1901 novel, *The First Men in the Moon*, which recounts the adventures of an eccentric inventor, Mr. Cavor, and his friend Mr. Bedford. Cavor invents a substance he names "cavorite" which essentially nullifies gravity. He builds a vehicle consisting of a glass sphere coated with cavorite, encased within a steel shell. The outer shell has movable louvers or blinds that can be opened

and closed to adjust the amount of gravity that can be nullified. Cavor and Bedford decide to journey to the moon using this conveyance.

Upon reaching the moon, the adventurers are discovered by the lunar inhabitants, a race of insect-like beings called "Selenites." The Selenites' chief activity is raising large larva-like creatures called "moon calves" for food. Cavor and Bedford are taken into caves below the moon's surface where they eventually meet the ruler of the Selenites, known as the "Grand Lunar," a being with a head and brain so large that it requires attendants to support its great size and weight—its body having shriveled into uselessness. At the end of the tale, Bedford returns to earth in the cavorite sphere, while Cavor remains behind to study the lunar civilization.

20. GEORGES MELIES SILENT FILM, *A TRIP TO THE MOON*

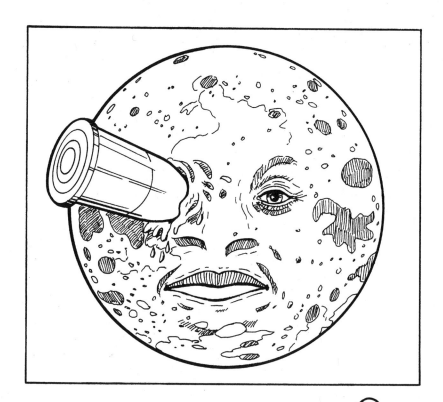

In 1902, French illusionist and filmmaker Georges Méliès (1861–1938) inaugurated the era of the science fiction film with his silent movie, *A Trip to the Moon.* Although crude and ridiculous in many ways, his first effort paved the way for the more thoughtful and sophisticated sci-fi films which would come later in the century. Melies' heroes are a group of scientists who journey to the moon in a hollow artillery shell fired from a giant cannon, much like the scenario in Verne's moon travel novels. The film's moon ship is shown striking the "man in the moon" in the eye, a special effect using an actor's face surrounded by a creme pie. Upon arriving at their destination, the scientists discover a race of crazed, primitive moon men who explode when struck by the scientists' umbrellas. Although by today's standards these kinds of visual effects are laughable, they were considered quite amazing at the time.

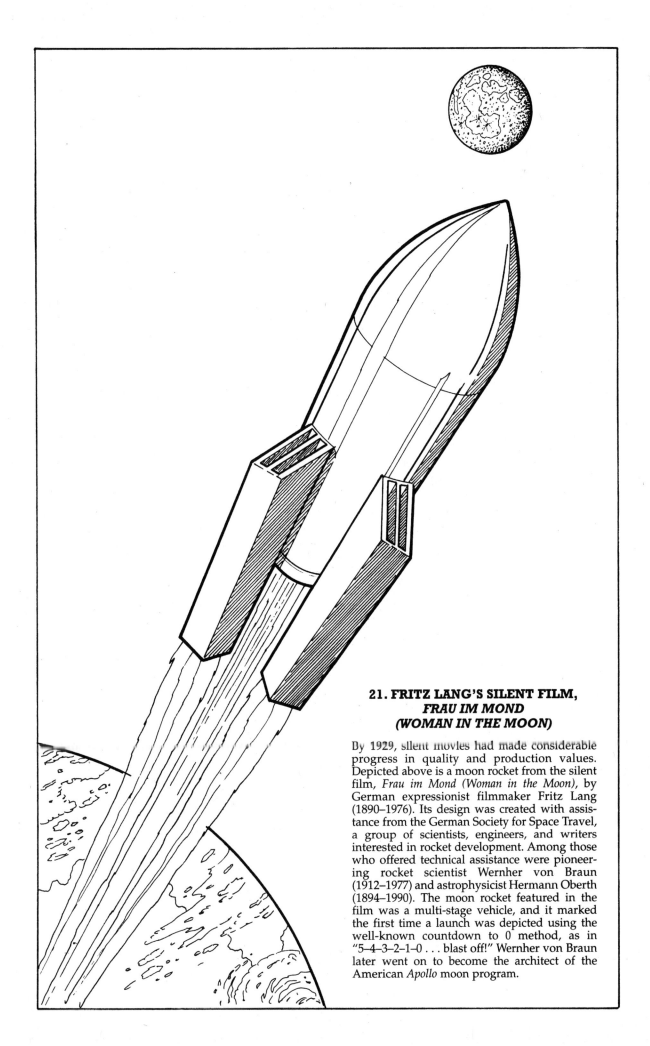

21. FRITZ LANG'S SILENT FILM, *FRAU IM MOND* *(WOMAN IN THE MOON)*

By 1929, silent movies had made considerable progress in quality and production values. Depicted above is a moon rocket from the silent film, *Frau im Mond (Woman in the Moon)*, by German expressionist filmmaker Fritz Lang (1890–1976). Its design was created with assistance from the German Society for Space Travel, a group of scientists, engineers, and writers interested in rocket development. Among those who offered technical assistance were pioneering rocket scientist Wernher von Braun (1912–1977) and astrophysicist Hermann Oberth (1894–1990). The moon rocket featured in the film was a multi-stage vehicle, and it marked the first time a launch was depicted using the well-known countdown to 0 method, as in "5–4–3–2–1–0 . . . blast off!" Wernher von Braun later went on to become the architect of the American *Apollo* moon program.

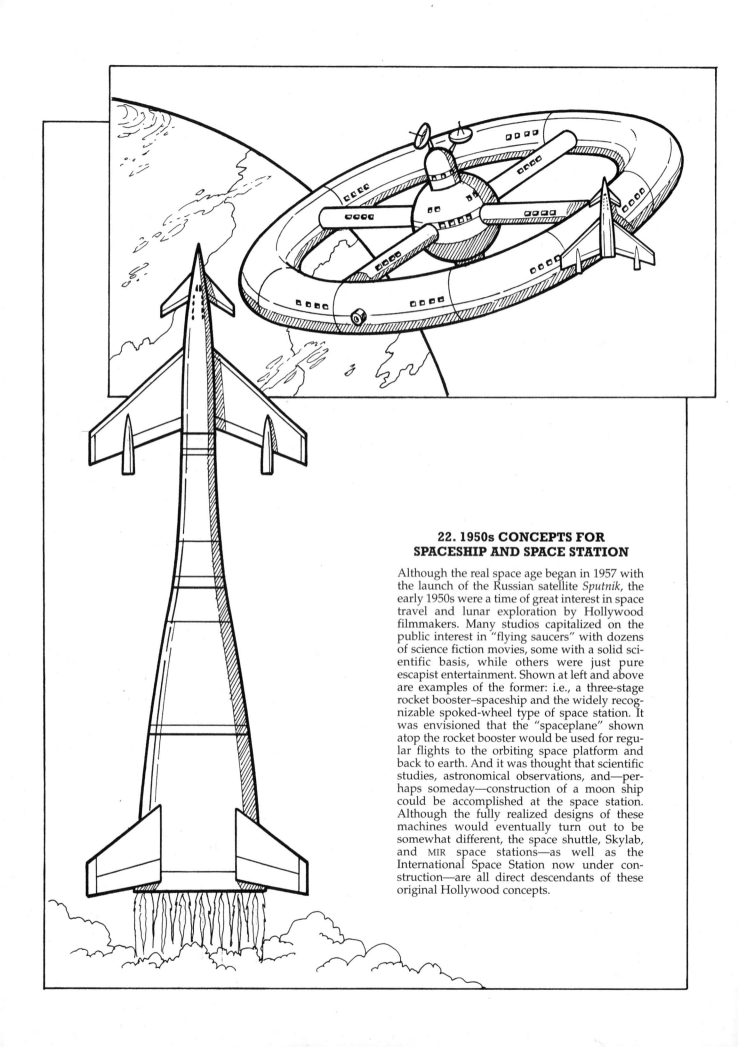

22. 1950s CONCEPTS FOR SPACESHIP AND SPACE STATION

Although the real space age began in 1957 with the launch of the Russian satellite *Sputnik*, the early 1950s were a time of great interest in space travel and lunar exploration by Hollywood filmmakers. Many studios capitalized on the public interest in "flying saucers" with dozens of science fiction movies, some with a solid scientific basis, while others were just pure escapist entertainment. Shown at left and above are examples of the former: i.e., a three-stage rocket booster–spaceship and the widely recognizable spoked-wheel type of space station. It was envisioned that the "spaceplane" shown atop the rocket booster would be used for regular flights to the orbiting space platform and back to earth. And it was thought that scientific studies, astronomical observations, and—perhaps someday—construction of a moon ship could be accomplished at the space station. Although the fully realized designs of these machines would eventually turn out to be somewhat different, the space shuttle, Skylab, and MIR space stations—as well as the International Space Station now under construction—are all direct descendants of these original Hollywood concepts.

23. 1950s CONCEPT OF LUNAR EXPLORATION

The picture above reflects the concept of moon exploration as it was envisioned based on the scientific knowledge of the early 1950s. The spaceship is the familiar sleek, winged bullet shape made popular during that time in countless science fiction films and television shows. It is very different from the *Eagle*, the actual lunar module which made the first historic landing on the moon in 1969 (depicted on page 32 of this book).

The lunar landscape as conceived at this time is covered with a dry, cracked terrain, punctuated by jagged mountains and rock outcroppings. We now know from the *Apollo*

lunar explorations that the moon's surface is softly rounded from the billions of years of impacts by micrometeorites which, in effect, "sand-blasted" the rocks, hills, and mountains into smoothly eroded shapes. As a result of this activity, the surface of the moon is covered with a fine talcum powder-like dust. The astronaut is shown wearing the then popular concept of a spacesuit featuring the familiar "accordion-fold" joints, an air tank much like a scuba diver's, and a tool belt festooned with useful devices. This imaginary projection is actually not far afield from the eventual *Apollo* moon spacesuit used in the 1970s.

24. RADAR MEN FROM THE MOON

At the other end of the spectrum from the 1950s science-based films about the moon, were those of pure fantasy made with little regard for the facts. Shown above is a scene from a popular movie serial made during the late 1940s and early 1950s called *Radar Men from the Moon*, and was part of a larger series starring "Commando Cody, Sky Marshall of the Universe." This stalwart defender of the earth battled Evil Retik, Ruler of the Moon, and his henchmen using his back-mounted rocket pack and trusty .45-caliber pistol. These serialized sci-fi shorts always ended with the Commando stuck in a seemingly deadly predicament, followed the next week by his miraculous escape. Short on plot, special effects, and acting quality, they nevertheless thrilled a generation of 1950s kids whose imaginations were sparked by the idea of rocketships and space travel adventures. Originally shown as serials in the late 1940s, they were repackaged and shown as a feature-length film in 1952. In addition to *Radar Men from the Moon*, the same studio—Republic Pictures—also put out two other Commando Cody movies, *King of the Rocket Men* and *Zombies of the Stratosphere*.

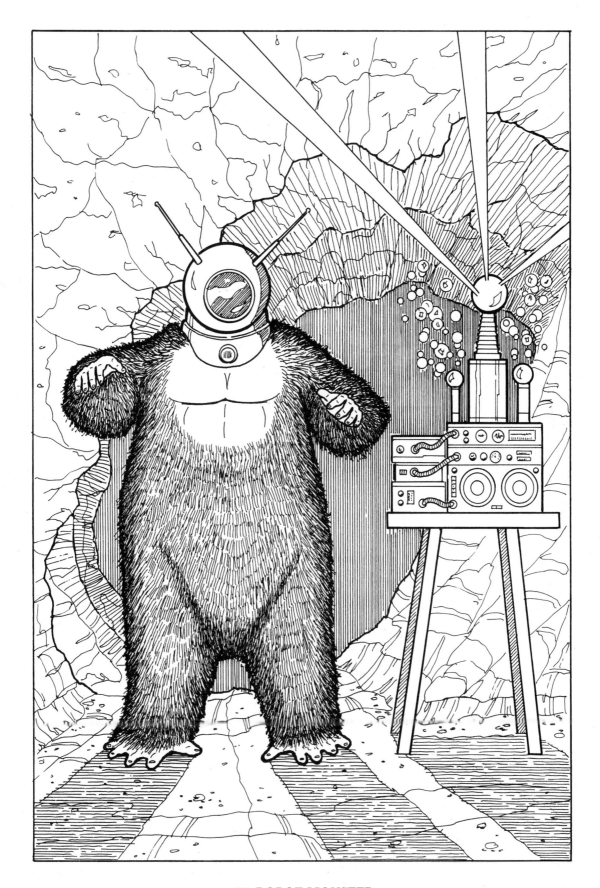

25. *ROBOT MONSTER*

Generally considered to be one of the worst, if not *the* worst, science fiction film ever produced is the plodding and absurd, *Robot Monster*, depicted above. Made on a shoestring budget in 1953, it stars an actor in a scruffy gorilla suit, topped by a diving helmet with the viewing port covered by a nylon stocking to hide the actor's face. "Ro-Man," as the creature is called in the film, is sent by his lunar leader, the "Great Guidance," to destroy all earthlings in preparation for colonization by his fellow moon apes. Ro-Man chases a group of embarrassed-looking actors around a dusty ravine and cave near Hollywood Boulevard, a location seen in a number of films of that era. The plot is inconsequential and the robot monster's yak-hair gorilla suit ludicrous, but if you're a fan of campy, cult films then *Robot Monster* is a must-see.

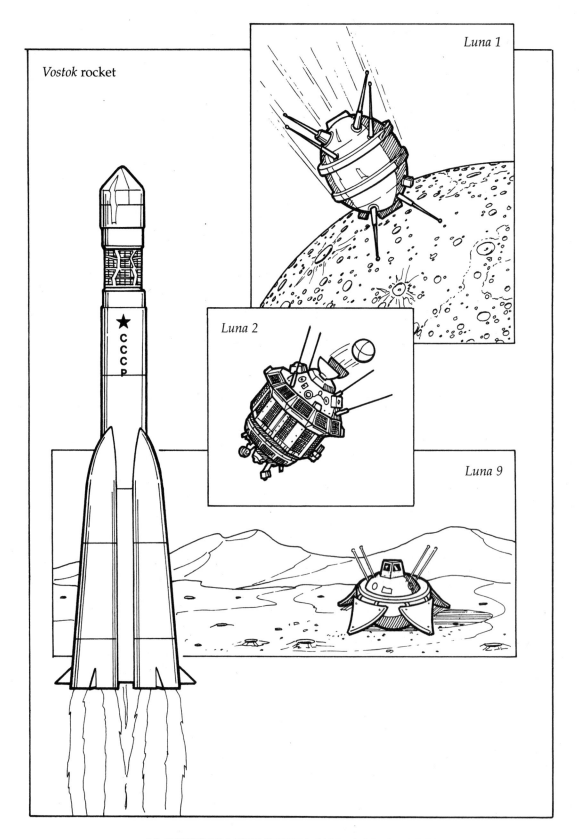

Vostok rocket

Luna 1

Luna 2

Luna 9

26. RUSSIAN *LUNA* SERIES OF MOON PROBES

The actual exploration of the moon began with unmanned space probes launched by Russia (then known as the Soviet Union) starting in 1959. Using their powerful *Vostok* rocket, converted from an Intercontinental Ballistic Missile (ICBM), the *Luna 1* probe became the first manmade object to leave the earth's gravity. Originally intended to impact the lunar surface, it missed the moon by 3,000 miles. The next Russian probe, *Luna 2*, was more successful, becoming the first spacecraft to reach the moon when it crashed onto its surface in September 12, 1959. An even more significant achieve-

ment was made by *Luna 3* (not pictured) in October of that same year. This little probe circled the moon and sent back the first-ever photographs of its far side.

The Russians continued their robotic exploration of the moon with other *Luna* series probes. In January of 1966, *Luna 9* achieved the first controlled landing by a spacecraft on the lunar surface. Although the main vehicle crash-landed on the moon, its ejected capsule landed safely, opened up its petal-like outer shell, and took the first panoramic close-up photos of the lunar terrain.

27. AMERICAN *RANGER* SERIES OF UNMANNED LUNAR PROBES

The American *Ranger* series of unmanned lunar probes began their exploration of the moon starting in 1961. These vehicles were designed to head straight into the moon, sending back data and pictures before they crashed. *Rangers 1* through 3 missed their target, but *Ranger 4* impacted on the moon's far side in April of 1962, becoming the first American spacecraft to reach the moon. *Ranger 7* relayed over 4,000 high-quality images back to earth before crashing on the lunar surface in July of 1964. *Ranger 9*, launched in March of 1965, was the last in this historic series of moon probes; it was sent to photograph a more complicated terrain than its predecessors and transmitted over 5,000 images during the final nineteen minutes before impact. The *Surveyor* series represented the next effort at lunar exploration with vehicles designed to soft-land on the moon's surface

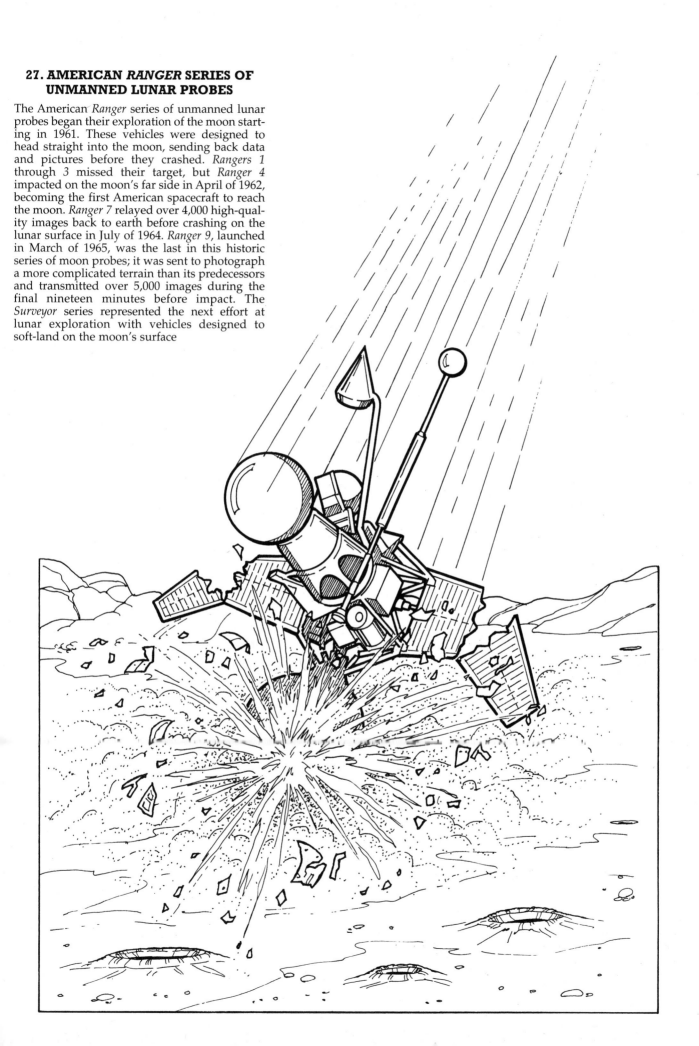

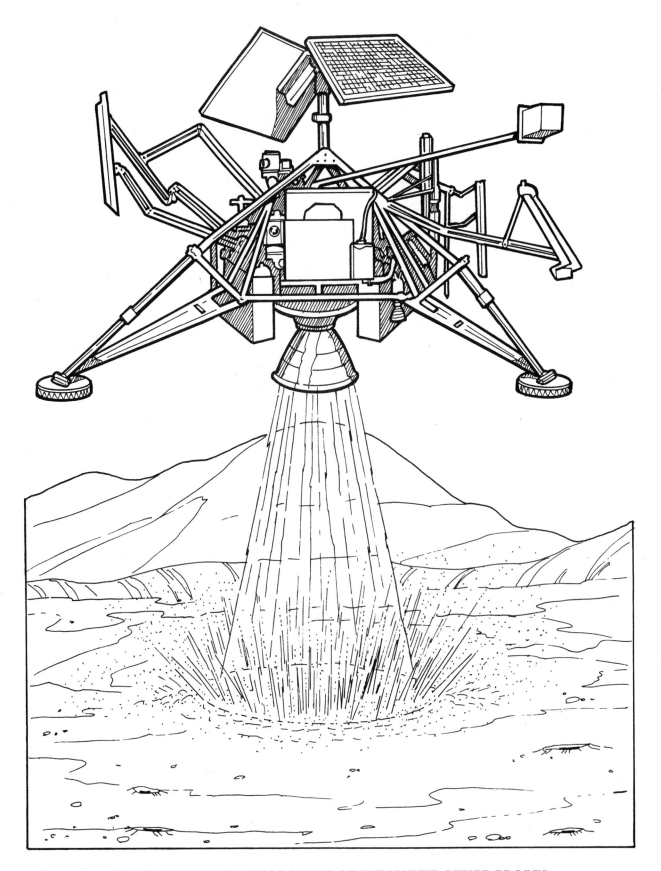

28. AMERICAN *SURVEYOR* SERIES OF UNMANNED LUNAR PROBES

The *Surveyor* series of soft-landing moon exploration space-craft began in 1966. These robotic probes were intended to land and take close-up photographs of the lunar landscape. They were also designed to scout out possible landing sites for a future manned lunar mission. On June 2, 1966, *Surveyor 1* made a successful controlled landing on the Ocean of Storms. Its camera transmitted over 11,000 images of the nearby landscape back to earth. When *Surveyor 3* landed on

a slope in April 1967, it bounced up and down a few times enabling the vehicle to photograph its own footprints, thus proving that the moon was not covered with too thick a layer of dust for human beings to be able to walk on its surface. Over the next two years, six more *Surveyors* were launched. The data they collected proved crucial indeed to mapping future landing sites for the *Apollo* program.

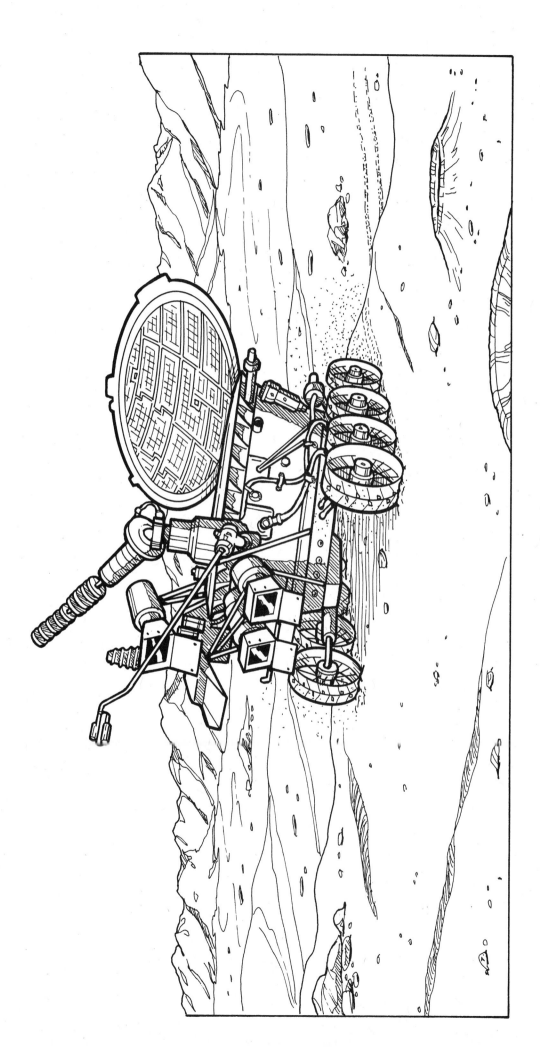

29. RUSSIAN *LUNOKHOD* ROBOTIC LUNAR ROVERS

The Russians landed two complex and sophisticated spacecraft on the moon in 1970 and 1973. These were the eight-wheeled roving vehicles, *Lunokhod 1* and 2, which were designed to explore the territory near their landing sites. *Lunokhod 1* spent more than ten months actively working on the moon and traveled a distance of six miles from its landing site; it returned more than 200 TV panoramas and 20,000 images. *Lunokhod 2* operated for four months, and roamed an even greater distance from where it landed—journeying twenty-three miles across the lunar surface; it returned 86 TV panoramas and 80,000 pictures.

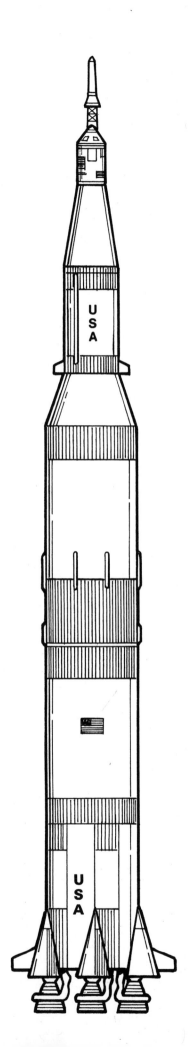
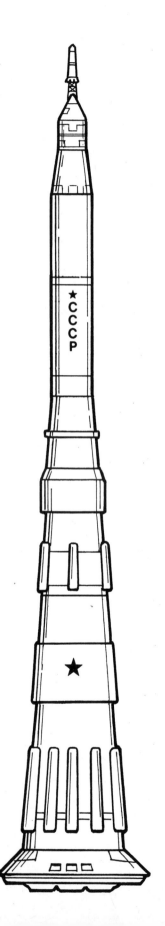

30. AMERICAN AND RUSSIAN MOON ROCKETS

The cold war between the United States and the Soviet Union lasted thirty years, finally ending with the collapse of the Soviet system in the early 1990s. Its primary manifestation was an arms race with each side striving to outdo the other in both the quantity and destructive power of their weapons. An offshoot of this competition was the space race, with the ultimate prize being the first manned mission to the moon.

Although the Soviets were first to launch an artificial earth satellite in 1957, and then to put a man—Yuri A. Gargarin—into orbit around the earth in 1961, the United States eventually caught up and surpassed the Russian efforts. Shown here are the two super-powerful rocket launch vehicles built for both the American and Soviet manned lunar missions. On the left is the mighty *Saturn 5* rocket used by the United States to successfully launch astronauts on six lunar landing missions. It stood 363 feet high with engines that created 7,750,000 pounds of thrust. On the right is the impressive Soviet N-1 moon rocket, the existence of which was not acknowledged until 1989. It stood 320 feet high and is estimated to have had engines producing 8 to 10 million pounds of thrust. It is believed to have been launched only once and exploded shortly after lift-off.

The Americans won the space race with their historic *Apollo 11* mission that carried three astronauts—Neil Armstrong, Edwin ("Buzz") Aldrin, and Michael Collins—to the moon and back. The Soviet manned lunar program was canceled soon after this American achievement. The Soviet Union's communist system—a secretive, bureaucratic dictatorship—could not prevail against the creative energy, economic power, and democratic organization of the United States.

31. AMERICAN *APOLLO 8* LUNAR ORBITING MISSION

The American manned missions to explore the moon were conducted by NASA (National Aeronautics and Space Administration) in their *Apollo* program. In 1968, a *Saturn 5* rocket launched *Apollo 8* on the first manned mission to orbit the moon. Three American astronauts—Frank Borman, James A. Lovell, Jr., William A. Anders—reached the moon on December 24, and completed ten orbits at a distance of just seventy miles above the lunar surface. They splashed

down into the Pacific Ocean on December 27.

The spacecraft shown above are the *Apollo* command and service modules, with the lunar module deployed at the tip of the command module, in position to begin the descent to the moon. The command and service module assembly is the vehicle in which the astronauts journeyed from the earth to the moon. During the lunar orbiting mission of *Apollo 8*, the lunar landing module was not included.

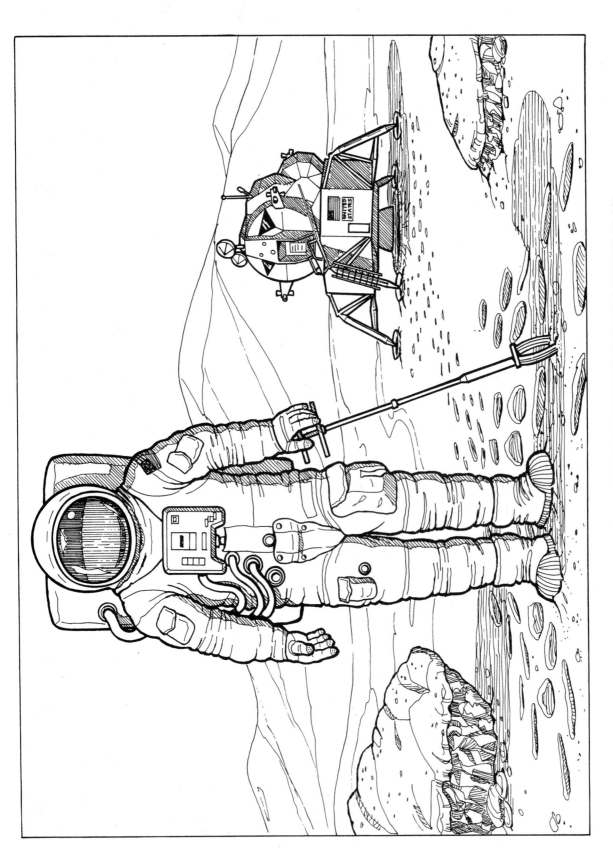

32. AMERICAN APOLLO 11 MISSION LANDS FIRST MEN ON THE MOON

Shown above is an American astronaut exploring the surface of the moon. This historic landing of human beings on another world occurred for the first time on July 20, 1969. The *Apollo 11* mission took astronauts Neil Armstrong, Buzz Aldrin, and Michael Collins on a spaceflight into the history books. Upon reaching the moon, Armstrong and Aldrin descended to its surface in the lunar module—nicknamed *Eagle*—while Collins remained in lunar orbit aboard the command module. The two astronauts explored the terrain around their landing site at the Sea of Tranquility for twenty-one hours before returning to the orbiting command module. There were five more successful lunar landing missions before the program ended in 1972.

33. *APOLLO MISSION, LUNAR ROVER*

During the moon missions of *Apollo 15, 16,* and *17,* the astronauts descended to the lunar surface carrying a compact, collapsible moon-mobile. This Lunar Roving Vehicle (LRV) could be set up and deployed to drive around their landing sites, powered by an electric battery, with an exploration range of fifty-seven miles.

On *Apollo 15* the astronauts traveled eighteen miles aboard the Rover to Hadley's Rille ("rilles" are large crevasses that crisscross the moon) and the surrounding Apennine Mountains. It was also during this mission that the astronauts tested Galileo's hypothesis of nearly 400 years before, that in the absence of air, any two objects would fall at the same rate of speed. The theory was confirmed as astronaut David R. Scott dropped a feather and a hammer, and observed them drop equally fast.

In April 1972, *Apollo 16* was launched toward the moon, targeting the area around the crater Descartes, to make the only highlands landing in a valley below high peaks. During *Apollo 17,* the Rover took them eighteen miles to explore the Taurus–Littrow region. The astronauts were able to transmit live television images of their expeditions using their on-board TV camera and dish antenna. The three Lunar Rovers remained on the moon after the astronauts departed, historical relics to be recovered someday by future moon explorers.

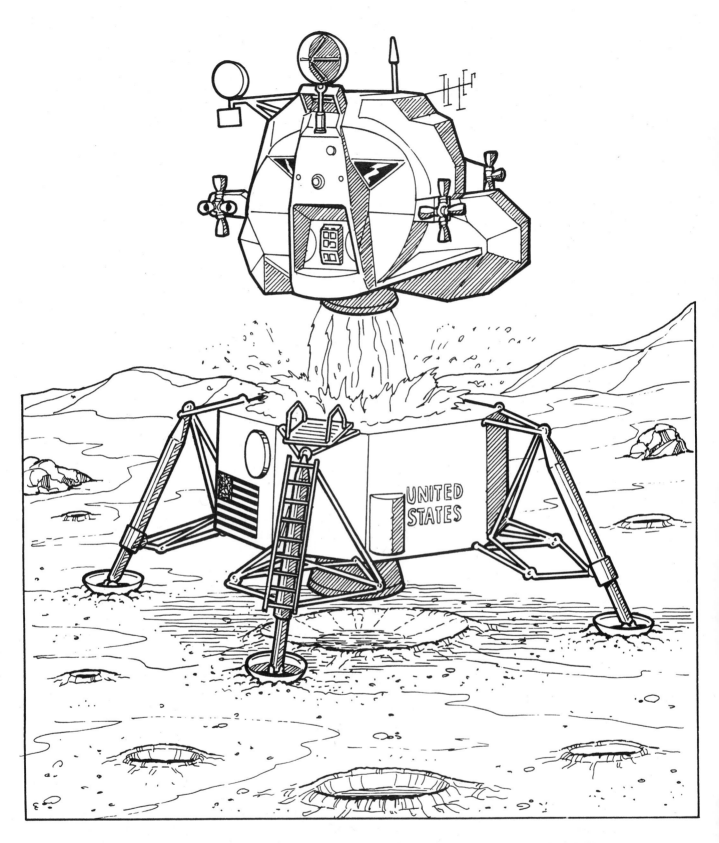

34. LUNAR MODULE ASCENT STAGE BLASTS OFF SURFACE OF THE MOON

The insect-like lunar module was constructed with two different joined sections. The bottom half of the vehicle was the "descent stage," and the upper half, the "ascent stage." The descent stage was used to land on the moon's surface using its rocket engine to gradually decrease its speed. Upon final approach, a soft landing was facilitated by the module's telescoping, shock absorbing legs. When the lunar mission was completed, the two astronauts lifted off aboard the ascent stage. This separated from the bottom portion of the lander using its own rocket engine, and then rejoined the command module already in lunar orbit. As with the Lunar Rovers, the five lunar module descent stages that landed on the moon remain, to be revisited one day by future astronauts.

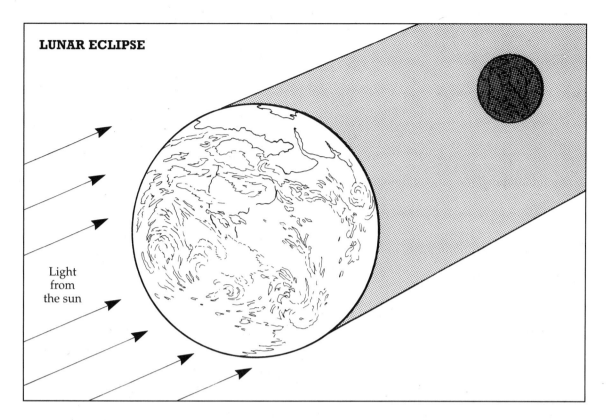

LUNAR ECLIPSE

Light
from
the sun

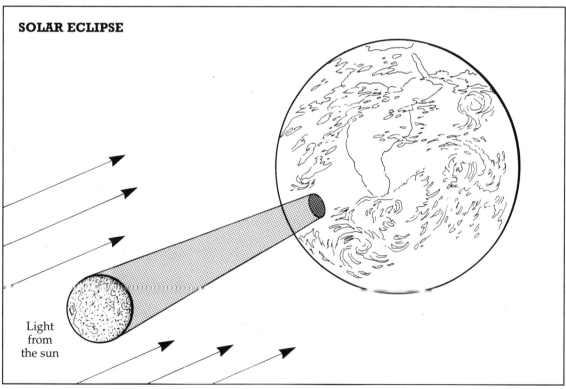

SOLAR ECLIPSE

Light
from
the sun

35. LUNAR AND SOLAR ECLIPSES

Depicted above are the periodic astronomical events called eclipses. The top panel shows an eclipse of the moon. In this occurrence, the moon moves into the earth's shadow, blocking the sunlight that reflects off the moon's bright surface. The earth's shadow begins as a narrow band of darkness at the edge of the moon, then gradually moves to cover the entire moon. However, the moon does not go completely black, since a small amount of light does continue to fall on the moon. As this reflected light enters the earth's atmosphere, only the red wavelength of visible light passes through which gives the moon a dark reddish-brown

appearance. Total eclipses of the moon occur approximately every two years.

The bottom panel shows an eclipse of the sun. In this event, the moon moves between the sun and the earth, casting its shadow on a portion of the earth. When the moon is at its closest position, around 217,000 miles from earth, the shadow is long enough to fall on a part of our planet. The largest circular eclipse shadow that can be cast upon the earth is 167 miles in diameter. Total eclipses of the sun also occur regularly, but far less often than lunar eclipses.

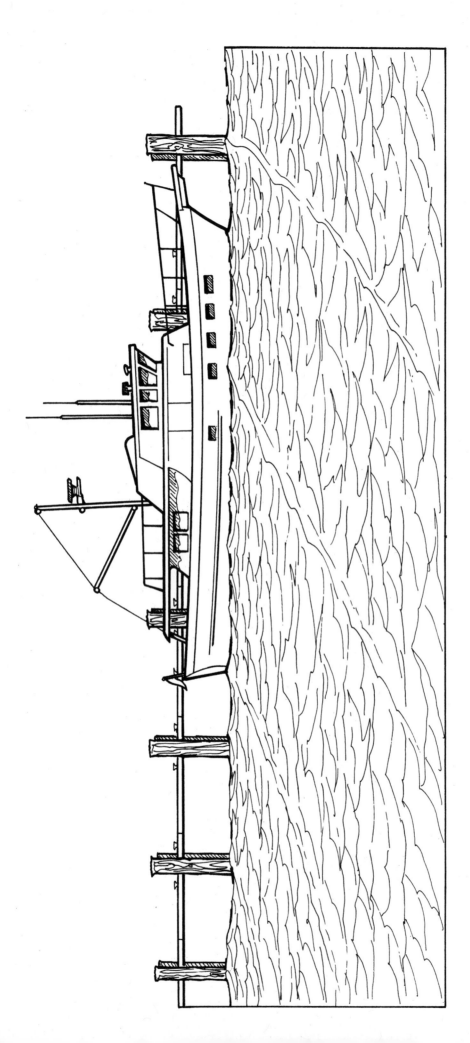

36. OCEAN TIDES

The close proximity to the earth of a large celestial body such as the moon has a number of readily observable effects. The most prominent of these physical consequences are the rising and falling of ocean tides. Two powerful forces act upon the earth's oceans to cause a rising and lowering of the depth of coastal waters on a daily basis. One force is the "gravity" of our moon, the other is "centrifugal force." Since the moon is a smaller body than the earth, its gravity is weaker. It nevertheless exerts a pull on the surface of our planet such that it does not revolve around the exact center of the planet. Rather, both the earth and moon revolve around a "balance point" between their gravities, located just beneath the earth's surface.

Because our planet is swinging around this balance point, a centrifugal force is created that causes movement in a direction away from the moon. The moon's gravity opposes this force, causing an imbalance between the part of the earth facing the moon and the far side of the moon. The oceans of the world reflect the irregular pull between these forces by bulging upward on the near side of the moon, thereby raising coastal water levels. This "high tide" occurs twice a day. As shown in the illustrations above and on the next page, some areas of the coastal ocean have more dramatic levels of tidal water depth variation than others. This difference is caused by the specific configuration of the local area geography, and by the natural movements of different ocean basins. The greatest depth variation occurs in the Bay of Fundy, Canada. Water levels can rise and fall as much as forty feet at this location, causing boats to peacefully float at high tide (as shown above), and yet become grounded in the mud at low tide (as shown on the next page).

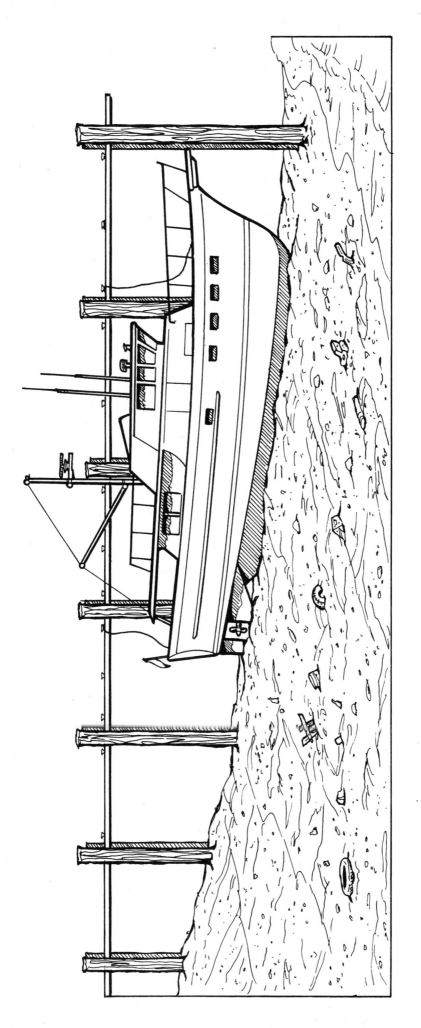

37. BAY OF FUNDY, CANADA, AT LOW TIDE

38. EFFECTS OF THE FULL MOON

The moon has long been a source of myth, legend, and folklore, especially when it shines with the brilliance of a full moon, inspiring stories both romantic and terrifying. For example, in some parts of Europe it was commonly believed that under the spell of a full moon, a man and woman would inevitably fall in love—i.e., become "moonstruck." Other myths allege the full moon can cause madness and insanity. In fact, the word "lunatic," meaning a demented person, is derived from "luna," the Latin word for the moon. In preparation for the anticipated effects of a full moon on its inmates, asylums in England would hire extra staff. And until the end of the nineteenth century, people who were accused of crimes committed during a full moon were generally treated with some leniency in consideration of its imagined influence.

One of the most famous legends about the full moon's effects concerns the "werewolf"—or "man-wolf." According to medieval superstition, a human being can be transformed into a wolf by the power of the rays of the full moon. There is an actual form of psychosis known as "lycanthropy," in which a person labors under the delusion that they have somehow acquired the characteristics of a wolf or other predatory animal. The term originates with Ovid's story of Lycaon, King of Arcadia, who was transformed into a wolf when he displeased the great god Jupiter (the Roman equivalent of Zeus). As depicted in books and movies, those bitten by a werewolf will themselves become one. The notion of a so-called "curse of the werewolf," was popularized by the 1941 Universal Pictures film *The Wolfman*.

39. INTERNATIONAL SPACE STATION

Currently under construction, the International Space Station is a multi-nation effort to create the largest orbiting science platform ever attempted. It is a shared project among the United States, Russia, Japan, Canada, Brazil, and the European Space Agency (consisting of eleven nations), and is expected to be complete and operational by 2004.

The station is designed around a central spine-like truss with various modular sections and solar panels emanating from this central core structure. The individual modules will be used for scientific experiments, habitation, power and maintenance, and storage. Different countries are constructing the various components of the station. All of the sub-assembled pieces will be launched into orbit aboard American space shuttles and Russian rocket boosters. These smaller sections will then be joined together in orbit by shuttle astronauts, eventually forming a single cohesive space station.

Far larger than the Russian MIR space platform currently in orbit, the new station will be 200 feet long and weigh over 1 million pounds. It will contain 46,000 square feet of living and interior workspace. There will be docking ports for the space shuttles, and even an emergency escape craft—looking much like a mini-shuttle—included as part of the station's standard equipment. As shown above, the International Space Station may also eventually be used as an assembly and departure point for the next generation of moon exploration spaceships.

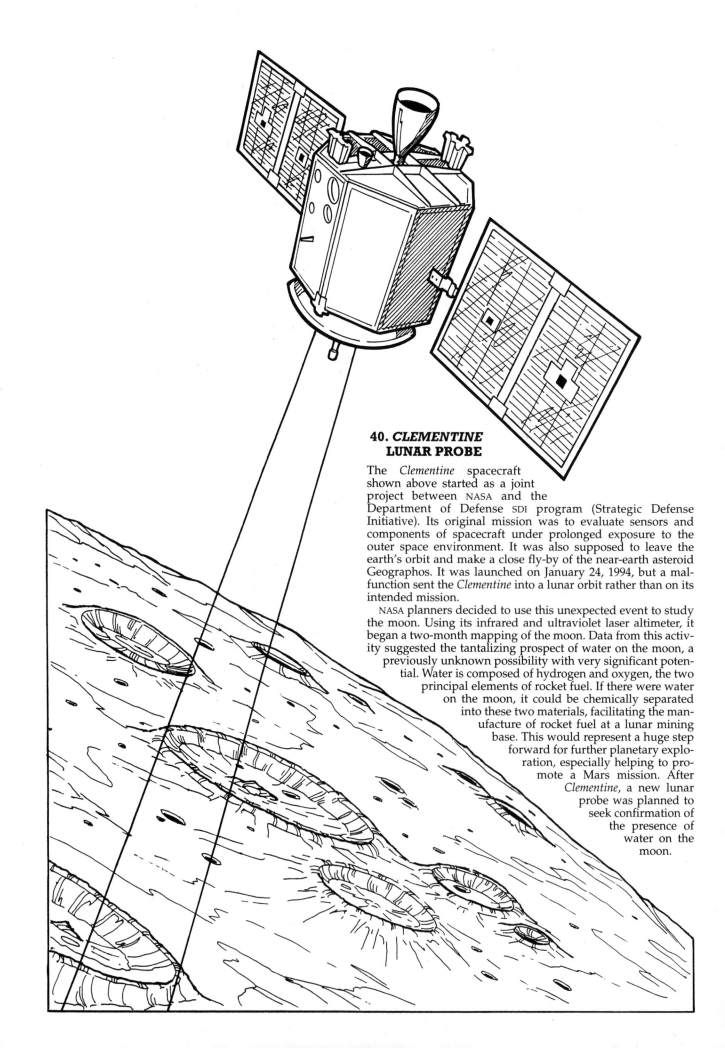

40. *CLEMENTINE* LUNAR PROBE

The *Clementine* spacecraft shown above started as a joint project between NASA and the Department of Defense SDI program (Strategic Defense Initiative). Its original mission was to evaluate sensors and components of spacecraft under prolonged exposure to the outer space environment. It was also supposed to leave the earth's orbit and make a close fly-by of the near-earth asteroid Geographos. It was launched on January 24, 1994, but a malfunction sent the *Clementine* into a lunar orbit rather than on its intended mission.

NASA planners decided to use this unexpected event to study the moon. Using its infrared and ultraviolet laser altimeter, it began a two-month mapping of the moon. Data from this activity suggested the tantalizing prospect of water on the moon, a previously unknown possibility with very significant potential. Water is composed of hydrogen and oxygen, the two principal elements of rocket fuel. If there were water on the moon, it could be chemically separated into these two materials, facilitating the manufacture of rocket fuel at a lunar mining base. This would represent a huge step forward for further planetary exploration, especially helping to promote a Mars mission. After *Clementine*, a new lunar probe was planned to seek confirmation of the presence of water on the moon.

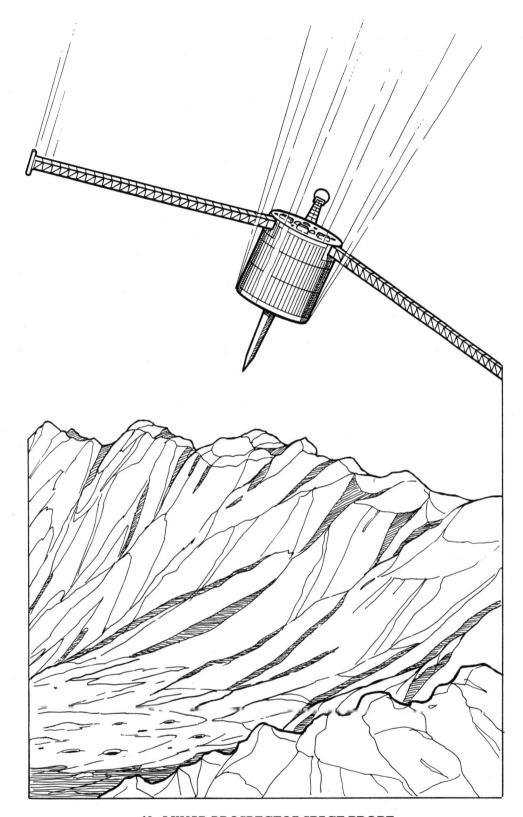

41. *LUNAR PROSPECTOR* SPACE PROBE

NASA designed the lunar probe *Prospector*, shown above, for the specific purpose of detecting water on the moon. Evidence collected by the Clementine probe suggested that frozen water (ice) may lie deep at the bottom of craters at the lunar south pole. If this evidence were confirmed, exciting possibilities could be exploited. Not only could the water be broken down into rocket fuel, but the oxygen and water could be used for life support by lunar explorers and colonists.

The 650-pound craft reached the moon in December 1998. The *Prospector* began orbiting the moon and analyzing its surface with a bevy of sophisticated instruments. An early examination of data that was gathered suggested the presence of up to 300 million metric tons of water, in the form of ice crystals, buried just eighteen inches below the lunar surface. The final event in *Prospector's* mission was to actually crash into a south polar crater with the intention of sending up a cloud of sub-surface debris that could be analyzed for traces of water by earth-based instruments. On July 31, 1999, *Prospector* impacted the moon at a potential water site. Unfortunately, results from the crash were inconclusive in determining the actual presence of water. It is expected that future moon exploration probes will answer this important question more definitively.

42. FUTURE MOON BASE MINING COLONY

It has been twenty-eight years since the last American astronaut explored the lunar surface. The new century will see a great expansion of exploration of the space frontier with missions to the moon and other planets, principally Mars. Depicted above is a possible configuration for a future moon base and mining colony. It would contain habitat structures, laboratories, power generation facilities, and mining equipment. Astronauts and scientists working on the surface would, of course, need to wear sophisticated spacesuits. They would have to be durable enough to protect lunar workers from the extremes of cold and heat. The temperature on the moon varies from −320 degrees below zero at night and in shaded areas, to +279 degrees in direct sunlight.

The principal material extracted from mining operations would be water in the form of ice. Believed to exist just below the lunar surface in massive quantities, ice crystals would be processed to separate its two constituent elements, hydrogen and oxygen, the ingredients for rocket fuel. Oxygen would be immensely useful to the moon colonists by supplying the air they need to breathe. The ice itself can be melted and refined into drinking water. The primary purpose of the lunar mine, however, would be to manufacture and store rocket fuel from the separated oxygen and hydrogen, thus allowing the moon to be a direct staging base for future planetary exploration.

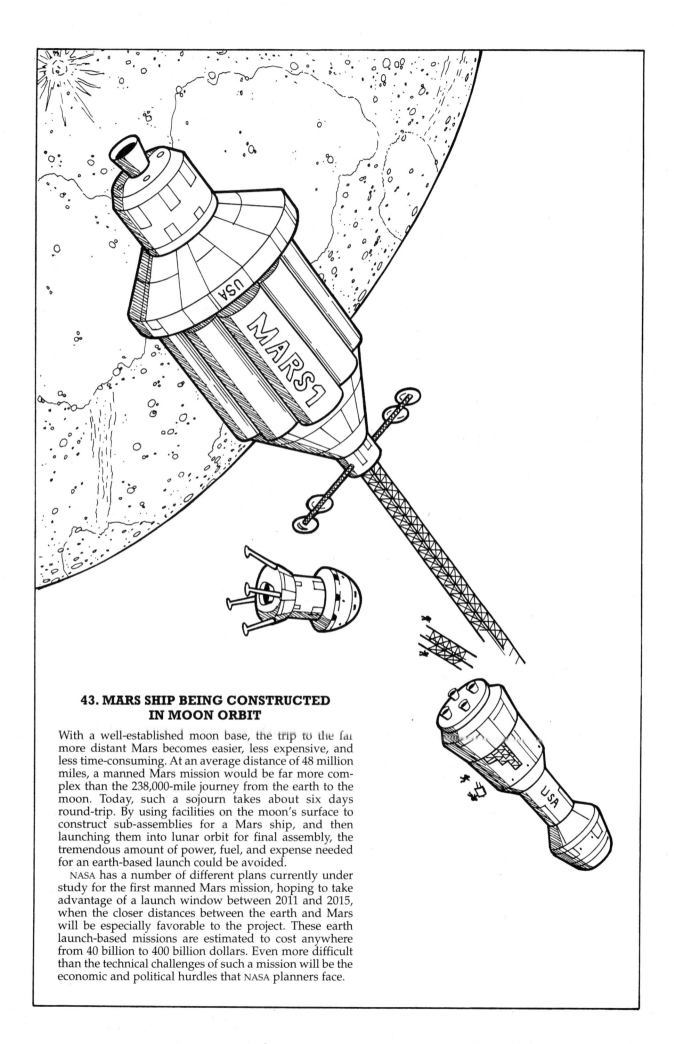

43. MARS SHIP BEING CONSTRUCTED
IN MOON ORBIT

With a well-established moon base, the trip to the far more distant Mars becomes easier, less expensive, and less time-consuming. At an average distance of 48 million miles, a manned Mars mission would be far more complex than the 238,000-mile journey from the earth to the moon. Today, such a sojourn takes about six days round-trip. By using facilities on the moon's surface to construct sub-assemblies for a Mars ship, and then launching them into lunar orbit for final assembly, the tremendous amount of power, fuel, and expense needed for an earth-based launch could be avoided.

NASA has a number of different plans currently under study for the first manned Mars mission, hoping to take advantage of a launch window between 2011 and 2015, when the closer distances between the earth and Mars will be especially favorable to the project. These earth launch-based missions are estimated to cost anywhere from 40 billion to 400 billion dollars. Even more difficult than the technical challenges of such a mission will be the economic and political hurdles that NASA planners face.

THREE SMALLEST PLANETS

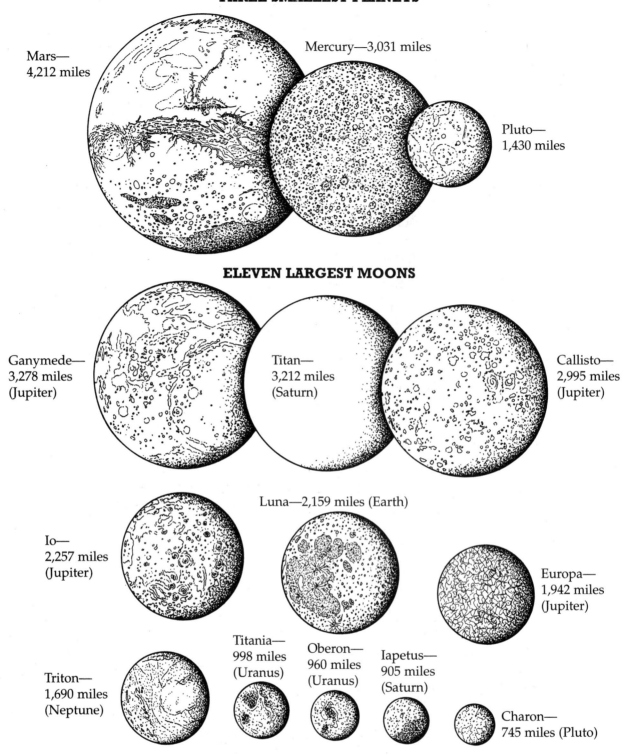

Mars—
4,212 miles

Mercury—3,031 miles

Pluto—
1,430 miles

ELEVEN LARGEST MOONS

Ganymede—
3,278 miles
(Jupiter)

Titan—
3,212 miles
(Saturn)

Callisto—
2,995 miles
(Jupiter)

Luna—2,159 miles (Earth)

Io—
2,257 miles
(Jupiter)

Europa—
1,942 miles
(Jupiter)

Triton—
1,690 miles
(Neptune)

Titania—
998 miles
(Uranus)

Oberon—
960 miles
(Uranus)

Iapetus—
905 miles
(Saturn)

Charon—
745 miles (Pluto)

44. MOONS OF THE SOLAR SYSTEM

There are dozens of moons orbiting the planets that make up our solar system. Saturn with its striking and complicated ring system, has the most numerous natural satellites, with more than twenty moons discovered. Giant Jupiter has sixteen moons circling its immense circumference. Depicted above are eleven of the largest moons in the solar system. They are drawn to scale in proportion with one another. Also shown at the top of the illustration are the three smallest planets, also drawn to scale for a size comparison with the various moons. As you can see, several of the moons are larger than the planets Mercury and Pluto. The largest moon is Jupiter's Ganymede, followed closely by Titan, the orange moon of Saturn. Callisto and Io circle Jupiter and are the next in size. Our moon is the fifth largest.

Several of the moons shown above exhibit very interesting features. Titan is completely shrouded by a dense orange-colored atmosphere of methane and nitrogen. It may have liquid methane rainfall that forms lakes, rivers, and perhaps even oceans. Jupiter's moon Io has numerous volcanoes spouting molten sulphur plumes that rise thousands of feet above the surface. Perhaps the most tantalizing moon in the solar system is Europa, one of Jupiter's many satellites. Europa's surface is completely covered with a cracked and fissured surface of ice. Scientists believe that Europa may have a warm water ocean beneath its icy crust. If the heat from the moon's interior warms the water sufficiently, there may be living organisms in Europa's sea. Future robotic probes to this fascinating world will eventually answer that question.